CW00516512

BRITI

A History from Beginning to End

Copyright © 2023 by Hourly History.

Table of Contents

Introduction

The British Raj refers to the time from 1858-1947 when Britain directly ruled the Indian subcontinent. During that 90-year period, India saw enormous social, political, and cultural upheaval. When the British first took control of this area, local rulers oversaw their own small kingdoms, which often had their own languages and social and religious traditions. Under British rule, new systems of education were introduced, and increasing industrialization brought societal change. The British administration also united large numbers of indigenous people, though they were often united mainly by their opposition to the British and in a desire for independence.

The growing independence movement also saw the emergence of one of the most influential and charismatic political leaders ever: Mahatma Gandhi. His policy of non-violent opposition inspired many leaders in other countries and helped to guide India to independence. However, with independence came partition; the British divided the region according to religious and ethnic lines. Instead of a single independent nation, the Indian subcontinent became two and then three separate nation-states, something that led to violence and conflicts that persist today. This is the story of how British rule inadvertently created the modern nations of India, Pakistan, and Bangladesh.

Chapter One

Background: Company Rule in India

"Educate the people of India, and govern them wisely, and gradually the distinctions of caste would disappear, and they would look upon us rather as benefactors than as conquerors."

—John Bright

When we think of globe-spanning mega-corporations, we most likely think in terms of modern companies such as Amazon, Facebook, or Apple. However, more than 400 years ago, a company was created that would go on to become one of the most powerful corporations in history. This company not only commanded a private army that was larger than the standing army of many nations, but it also conquered territory and crushed potential competitors to ensure that it controlled trade to Europe from India, China, Persia, and Indonesia for over 200 years.

It was on the very last day of the year 1600 that Queen Elizabeth I of England granted a charter to a group of merchants in London. Victory over the Spanish Armada had given English naval power a significant boost, but there was relatively little trade with distant lands. The merchants created a company—the Company of Merchants of London Trading into the East Indies (soon to be renamed the East India Company)—with the express purpose of establishing exclusive trade links over a huge area, stretching from Africa's Cape of Good Hope in the east to South America's Cape Horn in the west. One of the most potentially lucrative areas within this region was India.

While the new company had exclusive rights to trade on behalf of England, it initially faced determined competition from the French, Spanish, Portuguese, and Dutch, who had already begun to trade in this area. For that reason, the earliest East India Company outposts in India were protected by mercenaries employed by the company. These first outposts negotiated agreements with local rulers and, when required, provided well-equipped troops to fight on their side. The company prospered and grew until, by the eighteenth century, it had an army of a quarter of a million men; in comparison, the entire army of the British Empire at the same time numbered only a little over 100,000 troops.

In 1757, East India Company troops under the command of Robert Clive fought a much larger force from the Nawab of Bengal, supported by mercenaries from the French East India Company. This battle, called the Battle of Plassey, was part of the larger Seven Years' War (fought from 1756-1763). Clive was victorious, which left the East India Company in control of Bengal, one of the richest regions in India. Instead of being entirely focused on trade, the company became the de-facto ruler of Bengal, with responsibility for the collection of taxes. Recognizing how powerful this company had become in India, the British government passed the East India Company Act in 1784 which required that the governance of territory in India was shared between the company and the British Crown. In reality, though, this new act had little direct effect on the activities of the company, and the East India Company soon grew to become the largest trading company in the world.

The Industrial Revolution in Britain led to an increasing need for raw materials such as cotton from India, and by the end of the eighteenth century, the East India Company was reporting annual sales of well over £7 million, a staggering sum at that time. However, as the eighteenth century turned into the nineteenth, many people began to express concerns about the company and its role in the governance of India. New ideas gripped Britain, partly due to the writings of the Scottish philosopher and economist Adam Smith.

In 1776, Smith published an influential book entitled *An Inquiry into the Nature and Causes of the Wealth of Nations.* This work proposed what would now be called *laissez-faire* economic policies, allowing free markets to be governed by self-interest and competition. These theories, which became increasingly popular with economists and financiers, simply did not fit with the trade monopoly that the East India Company enjoyed. Thus, in 1813, the East India Company Act of 1813 renewed the company's charter and allowed it to rule in India but, crucially, ended its monopoly on all trade items except for tea.

In the middle of the nineteenth century, the armies of the East India Company in India numbered around 350,000 men: 50,000 British troops (mainly officers) supported by 300,000 "sepoys," Indians who served in the company's army. These troops were divided into three Presidency Armies based in Bombay, Madras, and Bengal.

By this time, there was widespread dissatisfaction amongst the sepoys in the East India Company Army. In Bengal, troops had been recruited on the understanding that they would not be required to travel further than they could march to fight. However, the East India Company's involvement in China—and particularly in the Opium Wars from 1839 to 1842—increased the requirement for troops who could be used overseas if required. This led to the adoption of the General Service Enlistment Act of 1856, which meant that any East India Company troops in India could be required to serve overseas. Another issue that caused dissatisfaction amongst sepoys was the lack of promotion prospects. British officers were generally favored, and it was difficult, if not impossible, for sepoys to achieve promotion to senior officer rank.

The final factor that pushed the sepoy armies over the edge and into mutiny and rebellion was the introduction of the new Enfield Pattern rifled musket as the standard infantry weapon for company troops. As with most contemporary muskets, ammunition for this weapon was provided in the form of a cartridge comprising powder and a lead ball wrapped in waterproof, greased paper. A soldier was required to cut the end off the cartridge, pour the powder down the barrel, and then ram the ball down on top. In order to make reloading as swift as possible, soldiers were expected to bite off the end of the paper cartridge.

Almost as soon as the new weapon was introduced, rumors began to spread that the grease used on the cartridges included both tallow (derived from beef and therefore offensive to Hindus) and lard (derived from pork and therefore objectionable to Muslims). Most sepoys were either Hindu or Muslim, and this issue was quickly recognized by the company as a potential source of trouble. One British officer noted, "Unless it be proven that the grease employed in these cartridges is not of a nature to offend or interfere with the prejudices of religion, it will be expedient not to issue them for test to Native corps."

In January 1857, an order was given that all cartridges made in India should be produced without grease so that soldiers could add their own acceptable form of grease. The musket reloading drill was also modified so that soldiers were permitted open the cartridges with their hands rather than biting them, if they chose. However, it seems that these new orders simply persuaded many sepoys that the original cartridges did contain both pig and cow fat.

Matters became critical on April 24 when 85 out of 90 sepoy troops of the 3rd Bengal Light Cavalry refused to perform firing drills. They were court-martialed on May 9, and most were sentenced to ten years imprisonment with hard labor. The following day, sepoy troops of the 3rd Bengal Light Cavalry attacked the prison in the city of Meerut in which their comrades were being held. A number of British officers were killed, and in the rioting that followed, 20 British and 50 Indian civilians were killed. The insurrection known as the Indian Mutiny (also the Sepoy Rebellion and the First Indian War of Independence) had begun.

The mutiny quickly spread to other parts of India. By the time that it was finally suppressed in 1859, around 6,000 British (out of a total of 40,000 then in India) had been killed. No one is certain how many Indians died, but most estimates suggest at least a quarter of a million. Many were civilians, massacred after the recapture of major cities. A letter published in the *Bombay Telegraph* noted, "All the city's people found within the walls of the city of Delhi when our troops entered were bayoneted on the spot, and the number was considerable, as you may suppose, when I tell you that in some houses forty and fifty people were hiding. These were not mutineers but residents of the city."

One young British officer serving in the East India Army at the time sent an anguished letter to his family, "The orders went out to shoot every soul. It was literally murder. I have seen many bloody and awful sights lately but such a one as I witnessed yesterday I pray I never see again."

Even before the mutiny was completely over, the British Parliament had decided that India was too valuable and too volatile to leave in the hands of a private company. Thus, in August 1858, the Parliament passed the India Act, which effectively abolished the East India Company's rights and responsibilities on the subcontinent. On November 1, a royal proclamation announced that henceforth, Queen Victoria would become empress of India and would assume responsibility for the government of India through the British secretary of state.

The British government immediately took over the administrative and taxing powers of the East India Company, took possession of its property, and all members of the mercenary army of the company were integrated into the British Army. From 1858, Britain would directly rule large parts of the Indian subcontinent, officially starting the period known as the British Raj.

Chapter Two

Beginning of British Crown Rule

*"The Government of India is the most arduous
and perhaps the noblest trust ever undertaken by
a nation."*

—William Ewart Gladstone

British rule began with an effort to try to
understand the roots of the rebellion that took
place in 1857/1858 in order to avoid a repetition.
The East India Company's efforts to introduce a
free market in the region were considered partly
to blame. This took no account of existing
cultures and undermined the existing hierarchical
society. The new administration made a
deliberate attempt to end this "westernization" of
the region and instead encouraged the integration
of rulers of semi-autonomous regions and high-
caste individuals to take part in government. The
imposition of direct British rule became

generally known as the British Raj; in the Sanskrit and Hindustani languages, the word *raj* approximately equates to "law" or "rule." In part, this reflected an attempt to be sympathetic to the feelings of local people.

The Raj was administered by a new office based in London, the India Office. This was an executive branch of the British government which operated alongside existing offices, including the War Office, Foreign Office, and Colonial Office. Despite its name, the new office was not just responsible for territory on the Indian subcontinent; it was also responsible for all British-controlled territory in Africa, South Asia, and the Middle East. In some ways, the India Office functioned in the same way as the East India Company had in the past, with the critical difference that it was controlled not by shareholders but directly by the British government through the secretary of state for India.

However, direct British rule did not apply to every area of India. In provinces in what became known as British India, the people were ruled directly by an administration headed by a British governor-general. In addition, over 500 so-called princely states were recognized by the British government. These were scattered across the subcontinent, and each had its own hereditary leader. These varied considerably in size. For example, Hyderabad, one of the largest princely states, covered more than 75,000 square miles (200,000 square kilometers), while over 200 of the smaller states covered areas of less than 10 square miles (25 square kilometers).

In theory, each princely state had the right to internal self-governance while their relationships with other states and countries were controlled by the British government, a situation known as suzerainty. Yet although each of these states was a nominally sovereign entity of the British Empire, the actual autonomy of each state was dependent on its size and power, and only a handful had their own government.

To oversee this complex and interlocking territory of the princely states and British India, the British government appointed a governor-general (also known as the viceroy of India) based in the city of Calcutta. The governor-general was directly answerable to the secretary of state for India. Operating beneath the governor-general was an executive council of five members. This council was already in existence when the British took control and had been used by the East India Company. However, by 1861, significant changes were made. Before that, decisions were taken collectively by the council, which proved complex and time-consuming. The Indian Councils Act of 1861 changed the role of the council to the portfolio system, where each member had responsibility for a specific aspect of governance.

When it was first created, the five members of the executive council were individually responsible for home, revenue, military, law, and finance. In 1874, a sixth member was added with responsibility for public works. However, the governor-general had the authority to overrule the council if necessary. All the standing members of the executive council were British, and all were appointed by the secretary of state for India. The governor-general also had the right to add up to six people of Indian descent to the executive council, though these took part only as advisors.

The 1861 act also included provisions for the creation of a legislative council, which would be responsible for the development of new laws. Six of the twelve members of this council were to be British, appointed by the secretary of state. The remaining six were to be of Indian descent, though they, too, acted only as advisors and had no voting rights. This was a small step, but it was the first time that people of Indian descent were allowed to take any part in the British governance of India. Indian members of the legislative council were carefully chosen; all were high-caste people, often wealthy landowners of rulers from the princely states, who were known to be loyal to the British Empire.

Each of the 11 provinces that formed British India also had its own appointed British governor. These were answerable to the governor-general, and each was expected to appoint a provincial executive council to advise on various topics. As required, provincial legislative councils were also formed, and again these included people of Indian descent who served in advisory roles. Although this was certainly an improvement on the situation compared to the previous rule of the East India Company when only British people served in government, the new system limited the participation of people of Indian descent to advisory roles, and those who were selected were generally chosen because they were known to be loyal to the empire. In that way, even with these new mechanisms in place, Indian people had very little influence on the governance of their own country. This fact was particularly apparent during times of trouble.

When crops failed in 1876/1877 on the Deccan Plateau, one of India's most important agricultural areas, the viceroy, Lord Bulwer-Lytton, continued to export grain to Britain. While millions of people starved in India, a record 320,000 tons of wheat were exported. It was unsurprising that many people—British and Indian—began to question how exactly India benefitted from being under such complete control by a foreign nation.

Chapter Three

The Indian National Congress

"Everyone knows that if the people of India could be unanimous for a day, they might sweep us from their country as dust before a whirlwind."

—Richard Burton

After the imposition of British rule, a number of changes were made. One of the most significant was the building of railroads and other infrastructure projects intended to improve economic development on the subcontinent. In 1858, there were under 200 miles (320 kilometers) of railroad tracks in India. Within ten years, this had expanded to more than 5,000 miles (8,000 kilometers), all built by British railway companies. These tracks mainly connected agricultural areas in the heartlands to British ports in Bombay, Madras, and Calcutta.

The rail links accelerated the extraction of raw materials from agricultural areas, which in turn led to a gradual transition from subsistence farming in many areas to the first truly commercial agricultural production. The railroads also led to the import of cheap commodities from Britain, which destroyed many local handicraft industries.

In education too, there were important changes. The English Education Act of 1835 had been introduced during the rule of the East India Company, partly at the urging of a man named Thomas Babington Macaulay, who believed that it was imperative that Indian children be offered an education. Macaulay believed in the innate superiority of western learning and technology and insisted that this could be taught only through the use of the English language. This, he claimed, would produce "a class of persons, Indian in blood and colour, but English in taste, in opinions, in morals and in intellect."

Many schools were opened by the East India Company and even, just before the rebellion in 1857, the first Indian universities. This program was continued after the imposition of direct British rule in 1858 (even today, English is taught in almost all schools in India), creating a new caste of Anglicized Indians. While the

British hoped that these people would be more amenable to accepting British rule, ironically, it actually led to a growing interest in some form of Indian independence.

The combined effects of improved education and increasing trade enabled by railways led to the creation of something relatively new in India: a middle-class of educated, literate people. Many of these people had passed through British-created universities and held senior positions in the vast Indian Civil Service. They began to question how they could play a more significant role in the government and engage in meaningful political dialogue with the British rulers of the Raj. Many were encouraged in 1867 when Canada was granted the status of dominion, giving it greater political autonomy from the British Empire. If this could be done in Canada, why not in India too?

Allan Octavian Hume was a British civil servant who had spent most of his life in India. He had been a senior administrator in the province of Etawah during the rebellion, which he felt was partly the outcome of mismanagement on the part of the East India Company. Hume continued to work in the Indian Civil Service under Crown rule, and after his retirement in 1879, he was free to pursue his two main interests: ornithology and helping to increase the role of people of Indian descent in the government of their own country.

Hume was concerned that a failure on the part of the British administration to address poverty in India and a continuing refusal to allow Indians to take part in governance might lead to another rebellion. He was also concerned about the dismissive attitudes of many senior members of the administration, stating that "a studied and invariable disregard, if not actually contempt for the opinions and feelings of our subjects, is at the present day the leading characteristic of our government in every branch of the administration."

Hume was largely ignored by the British establishment in India, though for a short time, he did have the support of the viceroy, Lord Dufferin. In 1885, Hume wrote an open letter to students at the University of Calcutta suggesting the creation of a new body, which he called the Indian National Congress, whose role would be to push for a greater Indian role in government. The first meeting of the new group was held in Bombay in December 1885, attended by Hume and 72 representatives from all the provinces in India. Here, Womesh Chunder Bonnerjee was elected to be the first president of the new group.

Hume left India in 1894 and returned to live in England, but the movement he had helped to create would go on to be a significant factor in Indian politics.

Chapter Four

The Partition of Bengal

"There may be religious difference between us. There may be social difference between us. But there is a common platform where we may all meet, the platform of our country's welfare."

—Surendranath Banerjee

For the first twenty years of its existence, the Indian National Congress was little more than a forum for debate. Nevertheless, it did help to change the political landscape in India. It provided a platform for those Nationalists who believed that the British Raj, far from improving living conditions for the majority of Indians, actually made them worse by using taxes to pay the substantial salaries of senior civil servants.

By 1900, the Congress was becoming more politically active, though it was also increasingly split between moderates and extremists. One of the most active moderates was Gopal Krishna Gokhale, who was opposed to agitation but formed the Servants of India Society, which lobbied for political reform. Many extremists meanwhile gathered around Bal Gangadhar Tilak, who not only promoted agitation against British rule but also founded an explicitly Hindu political movement.

During this time, the British viceroy of India was Lord Curzon, who energetically pursued reforms to increase efficiency in the bloated civil service. However, one of his reforms proved massively controversial. The largest province in British India was Bengal. The population of the western part of this province was largely Hindu, while the population in the east was majority Muslim. To enable more efficient governance, Curzon announced that Bengal would, in 1905, be divided into two new provinces: Muslim-majority East Bengal and Hindu-majority West Bengal. To Curzon, this seemed to be no more than a logical response to an existing situation, but it provoked fury amongst many people.

The wealthy Hindu landowners in West Bengal found themselves separated from lands they owned in East Bengal, which they now forced to lease to Muslim peasants. Many people who belonged to the Indian National

Congress (which was dominated by Hindus) objected strongly to the creation of a new Muslim-majority province. Opposition to the partition of Bengal was led within the Congress by one of its founding members, Surendranath Banerjee. Banerjee created the Swadeshi ("buy Indian") movement to organize opposition to the partition. This involved a boycott of buying any British goods and the social isolation of any Indian who purchased foreign goods. These protests spread across India, and there were blockades of schools on the day of the partition and demonstrations in a number of Indian cities. The Swadeshi movement led to a decrease in the import of British cloth by about 25%. Wearing clothes made from Indian-manufactured fabric became a badge of protest for Hindus across India.

The partition also led directly to the creation of the All-India Muslim League in 1906. Many Muslims supported the partition of Bengal because it created India's first Muslim-majority province. For many Muslims, the creation of such a state seemed to be the only way for Muslims to achieve any level of political power in India. The British administration thus found itself caught between two opposed factions: members of the Indian National Congress who were absolutely opposed to the partition of Bengal and members of the All-India Muslim League who wanted to keep it in place. In the end, the continuing protests and the impact of the boycott on British goods proved decisive; the partition was rescinded in 1911.

Nevertheless, this crisis had led to two important developments: Muslims had formed their first national group in India, and the Indian National Congress had discovered that concerted action could persuade the British administration to change course. Even as the fallout from this debacle was becoming apparent to all, a global conflict was about to begin, which would forever change Britain's place in the world and its relationship with India.

Chapter Five

World War I

"I do not wish the war to end soon. I should like to die in this country and I have no intention of returning to India. . . . May the Holy Guru save me from India?"

—Sowar Natha Singh

In early August 1914, Britain and its allies found themselves at war against the German and Austro-Hungarian Empires. From the very beginning of World War I, Britain was critically short of troops. The professional British Army had fewer than 250,000 soldiers (and that total included troops serving overseas); in comparison, the army of the German Empire comprised almost four million troops. Britain had always focused resources on its navy—the Royal Navy was still the most powerful in the world—but the advent of a new land war in Europe meant that Britain urgently needed additional ground troops.

Indian troops were sent to the Western Front as early as October 1914. For the next twelve months, these troops would participate in every major battle in which the British Army was involved, including the First and Second Battles of Ypres, as well as the Battles of Neuve Chapelle, Aubers Ridge, and Loos. Subedar Khudadad Khan became the first Indian recipient of the Victoria Cross, Britain's highest award for valor, in October.

During the war, over one million Indian troops would serve with the British Army in Flanders, Gallipoli, and the Middle East. About 75,000 were killed and over 60,000 wounded. The contribution of Indian troops, particularly in the early battles on the Western Front, was critical. Later, Field-Marshal Claude Auchinleck, commander-in-chief of the Indian Army, would later write that Britain "couldn't have come through World War I . . . if they hadn't had the Indian Army."

Even while large numbers of Indian troops were fighting to preserve the British Empire, new independence movements were gaining support at home. Lala Har Dayal was an Indian who lived in America and worked as a professor at Stanford University. He initially worked to help Indian immigrants in the U.S., but soon he became interested in the overthrow of the British Raj. He believed that a popular revolution in India could achieve independence, and he began to tell Indian immigrants in America that they should return home and start working toward that end. This movement, which became known as the Ghadar movement, took its name from an Indian newspaper published in America, the *Hindustan Ghadar*.

The Ghadar movement in India was led by Rash Behari Bose, a revolutionary who had been involved in a failed attempt to assassinate the viceroy, Lord Hardinge. Ghadar activists secretly infiltrated Indian Army units during the early part of 1915. Bose and others hoped that a mutiny by the Indian Army could precipitate a revolution. In the end, however, these efforts failed; most of the Ghadar leaders in India were arrested, and 45 were executed. Bose himself fled to Japan.

The Ghadar movement wasn't the only group in India working toward independence. Bal Gangadhar Tilak, one of the founder members of the Indian National Congress, had spent time imprisoned in Burma before returning to India in 1915. He too wanted independence, but instead of a violent revolution, he advocated gradual reform of the administrative system to increase the participation of Indians. He also specifically condemned violent attacks on the British and encouraged his followers to support Britain during World War I.

Tilak's efforts seemed to have worked when, on August 20, 1917, the secretary of state for India, Edwin Montagu, made an important announcement. Henceforth, he claimed, a higher proportion of people of Indian descent would be involved in the administration of the country. He went on to say that this was being done as a precursor to the creation of some form of self-rule. The announcement caused celebrations amongst Tilak's followers; it seemed to hint that, once the war was over, India could expect to begin the process of self-government.

However, Montagu's statement included a significant clause that many ignored in the euphoria of the moment—only the British government had the right to decide when self-government might be done and what form it would take. Many Indian Nationalists assumed that it would happen quickly, but once the war was over, it became clear that the British had a much longer-term transition in mind. It would take a new leader to once again push the question of Indian self-rule back to the forefront of politics in India and Britain.

Chapter Six

Mahatma Gandhi

"We are our own slaves, not of the British. This should be engraved on our minds. The whites cannot remain if we do not want them. If the idea is to drive them out with firearms, let every Indian consider what precious little profit Europe has found in these."

—Mahatma Gandhi

Mohandas Karamchand Gandhi would become the best-known exponent of Indian independence and one of the most renowned people in the world under the name he was later given: *Mahatma* ("venerable") Gandhi.

Gandhi was born in October 1869 as a member of a Gujarati Hindu Modh Bania family in the town of Porbandar, then part of the princely state of Porbandar. In 1888, he moved to London, where he studied law at the University of London. He returned to India in 1891 and set up a law practice in Bombay. This venture failed, and in 1893, Gandhi moved with his family to South Africa (then part of the British Empire), where he took a position as a lawyer for a large shipping company. He expected to remain in South Africa for one year. Instead, he spent the next 21 years in that country.

Before his arrival in South Africa, Gandhi seems to have been a supporter of the British Empire, but the racial and religious discrimination he saw there would change his views. He became involved in politics and helped to found the Natal Indian Congress in 1894. Through this organization, he campaigned for the rights of the Indian community in South Africa. He became so successful in this, and so well known, that in 1897 he was attacked by a violent mob of white South Africans. He was saved from injury or even death only by the intervention of the police.

During the Boer War, Gandhi created the Natal Indian Ambulance Corps, a group of Indian volunteers who supported the British Army with medical facilities during that war. Gandhi and 37 other members of the corps received the Queen's South Africa Medal as a result of their actions. In 1906, however, the Transvaal government (the British administration in South Africa) introduced a new act that required the registration of all Indian and Chinese people in the colony. Gandhi saw this as discrimination and organized protests against the act.

For the first time, these protests involved a new approach devised by Gandhi: *Satyagraha*. This approach (the name means "holding firmly to truth") involved non-violent protest and passive resistance. Gandhi later said of this approach, "Truth (*satya*) implies love, and firmness (*agraha*) engenders and therefore serves as a synonym for force. I thus began to call the Indian movement Satyagraha, that is to say, the Force which is born of Truth and Love or non-violence."

In 1915, Gandhi returned to India, bringing with him the new ideas of Satyagraha. For one year, he did not join any political organization or take part in any political events. Rather, he spent this time traveling across the country, meeting with ordinary Indians and gaining a deep understanding of the situation there. It was not until 1917 and 1918 that he became involved in a number of protest actions to support local groups. The most notable was in the province of Kheda, where peasants were struggling in the face of increased taxation needed by the British government to support the war effort. Gandhi led these peasants in a wave of non-violent protest that led to concessions from the government, though as part of the final agreement, Gandhi was forced to agree not to publicize this victory. Despite this, Gandhi's fame within India was growing, and people, especially the young, were increasingly attracted by his approach of strength through peace and pacifism.

In 1919, Gandhi organized large-scale protests against the Rowlatt Act, a state of emergency installed in India to limit civil liberties and restrict rights to protest. These had been brought in during World War I as a response to the Ghadar movement, but with the war over, Gandhi and his growing number of followers believed that the act should be repealed. A nationwide Satyagraha began on April 6, 1919. Unfortunately, to Gandhi's horror, these protests became violent in many Indian cities, including Delhi.

In the Punjab, where ordinary people had suffered particularly severely during the war, the protests were notably large and violent. Gandhi planned to travel to the Punjab to try to persuade his followers to adhere more closely to the precepts of Satyagraha, but as he did, he was arrested by the British and sent to the city of

Bombay. While in Bombay, Gandhi and his followers would learn of a terrible massacre carried out by British troops.

Chapter Seven

Massacres and Non-Cooperation

"I believe strongly that where there is a revolutionary element expressed in action, one must act resolutely."

—Lord Birkenhead

The Golden Temple complex in the city of Amritsar in the Punjab had been the focus of large religious celebrations by Hindus and Sikhs for hundreds of years. However, when the Satyagraha protests in that city turned violent, the local British military commander, Brigadier-General Reginald Dyer, banned all public meetings. Despite this ban, large numbers of people began to gather near the temple on April 13, 1919, for the festival of Vaisakhi.

By five o'clock in the evening, an estimated 6,000 people were gathered in the Jallianwala Bagh, a walled garden close to the temple. Many were on their way home when Dyer and around 50 troops arrived. Without giving any warning, Dyer ordered the exits from the garden blocked and then told his men to open fire. He later said that this was done "not to disperse the meeting but to punish the Indians for disobedience." For ten minutes, troops fired at the unarmed crowd, stopping only when they began to run short of ammunition. Estimates of the number of dead vary, but it is likely that 1,000 civilians were killed either by gunfire or in stampedes as people tried to escape. This included a number of children, with the youngest being a baby of seven months. Over 1,000 more people were wounded.

Dyer submitted a report which claimed that his men had been faced "by a revolutionary army." There does not seem to have been any truth in this. These were civilians, including the elderly, women, and children, who had attended the festival at the Golden Temple complex. There is no evidence that any were armed or that they posed any kind of threat to British troops. On receiving Dyer's report, his commanding officer, Major General William Beynon replied, "Your action was correct and Lieutenant Governor approves."

However, not everyone in Britain agreed. Winston Churchill called the massacre "unutterably monstrous" and, in a House of Commons debate in 1920, told members of Parliament, "The crowd was unarmed, except with bludgeons. It was not attacking anybody or anything. . . . When fire had been opened upon it to disperse it, it tried to run away. Pinned up in a narrow place considerably smaller than Trafalgar Square, with hardly any exits, and packed together so that one bullet would drive through three or four bodies, the people ran madly this way and the other."

In India, an executive council decided that Dyer had acted in a "callous and brutal way," but because his actions had been condoned by his military superiors, he could not be prosecuted for his actions. The only repercussion was that he was relieved of his command on March 23 and prohibited from future employment by the British Army in India.

The massacre in Amritsar horrified Gandhi and his followers. He became more certain than ever that non-violent protest through Satyagraha was the only way to apply pressure on the British administration without putting lives at risk. He thus started a non-cooperation movement intended to spread Satyagraha across India.

Many members of the Indian National Congress had become disillusioned by the fact that Britain seemed to have no intention of fulfilling the promises made in the Montagu announcement. Many were also revolted by the massacre at Amritsar, and large numbers began to join Gandhi's movement.

The non-cooperation movement was officially launched on August 1, 1919, and involved a boycott of British schools, goods, and taxes. In the first month alone, over 90,000 students left British schools. On September 4, the Indian National Congress officially joined the movement. Many members of the Congress renounced the titles and honors they had been awarded by the British administration. Large groups gathered to burn British clothes and other goods.

The British responded by arresting up to 30,000 people across India, though Gandhi was left free. The movement continued until another incident in February 1922. In the small town of Chauri Chaura in the United Provinces, protestors set fire to a police station, killing more than twenty officers. Disappointed by the violence, Gandhi ordered the end of the non-cooperation movement. Soon after, he was arrested and sentenced to six years in prison for sedition.

Chapter Eight

The Government of India Act

"Freedom is my birthright. I must have it."

—Bal Gangadhar Tilak

Gandhi was released from prison in February 1924, having served only two years. The non-cooperation movement then resumed in the mid-1920s. In 1930, Gandhi led the Salt Satyagraha, in which many thousands of Indians protested against British taxes on salt by marching to the sea and making their own salt by evaporating seawater.

Gandhi's movement led hundreds of thousands of Indians to boycott British goods (which caused major problems for British firms trading with India). He also encouraged his followers to refuse to take any part in the British administration of India, which led to significant problems for the Indian Civil Service (ICS).

Joining this organization had become significantly less attractive to British people following widespread coverage of events such as the Amritsar massacre and the protests and non-cooperation that followed. Gandhi's growing influence meant that fewer Indians were willing to join, and the ICS began to struggle to fulfill their responsibilities. This was a particular problem in relation to the collection of taxes. The British administration in India was funded through these taxes, and if these could not be reliably collected, the whole financial basis of British rule would be under threat.

Partly in response to these problems, the British passed the Government of India Act in 1935. This act authorized for the first time the establishment of independent legislative assemblies in all provinces of British India. It also mandated the formation of a central government incorporating all the provinces of India. Elections to the national government would be held in 1937.

The Indian National Congress made a concerted effort to increase its membership in the period leading to the election. Its membership in 1935 was around 400,000; by 1939, it had over four and a half million members. As a result, the Indian National Congress took control of seven of the eleven provinces of British India after the elections. The Muslim League, representing Muslim minorities in several provinces, also performed well. This was a stunning and unwelcome surprise to the British, who had believed that the Muslim League and the Congress were elite organizations with relatively little popular support.

As new Congress governments were formed in these seven provinces, people of Indian descent had a real and significant role in the governance of their country for the first time since the British occupation. However, these changes in India were soon overshadowed by international developments that led to a new world war.

Chapter Nine

World War II

"Give me blood, and I shall give you freedom!"

—Subhas Chandra Bose

World War II began in September 1939 when Britain and France declared war on Nazi Germany. The viceroy in India, Lord Linlithgow, immediately also declared war on Germany without consulting any of the provincial governments. Infuriated by what they saw as a willful disregard for the powers they had been promised, all the provincial Congress governments resigned in protest.

Despite this, over two million Indians volunteered to serve in the British Army in World War II. The war also had a significant and positive effect on the economy of the country. The British government bore the cost of Indians serving in the army, and Indian industry made vast profits from the production of war materials, including ammunition, uniforms, rifles, machine guns, and artillery. When the war bcgan, India had a significant national debt, but by the time the war ended, it had a surplus of over £1 billion.

Nevertheless, many Indian Nationalists saw the war as an opportunity to advance their cause. Some continued to recommend a policy of non-cooperation, and in response, the British government sent a delegation to India to discuss the possibility of independence in return for full cooperation. The Cripps mission arrived in India in March 1942 but failed to reach any agreement with the Nationalists. The mission promised complete Indian independence after the war in return for full backing for the war effort, but by now, many Indians were wary of British promises.

As a result of the failure of these talks, in July 1942, the Indian National Congress launched the Quit India movement, a new campaign of civil disobedience and non-cooperation. The British responded in August by arresting and imprisoning every national and provincial Congress leader, including Gandhi. Tens of thousands of people would remain in prison for the remainder of the war.

The British administration was dismayed when these arrests did not stop the Quit India movement. Instead, in many cities, including

Bombay, Delhi, Allahabad, and Kanpur, people organized mass protests and defied British laws. Bridges were blown up, and telephone and telegraph lines were cut; these were seen as symbols of British rule and were targeted deliberately. Students quit their studies, and many began to produce illegal newspapers since the British had banned all mention of the Quit India movement in the mainstream press. Police and army units opened fire on groups of protestors, killing large numbers. In some cases, RAF aircraft were used to strafe large gatherings.

One former president of the Congress, Subhas Chandra Bose, went even further. Bose had managed to escape from India before the mass arrests, and he sought the help of the Japanese Empire to achieve Indian independence. He formed the Indian National Army to fight against the British and on behalf of the Japanese. Many of these were former Indian British Army troops who had been captured by the Japanese. This army made relatively little contribution to the war in Asia, and in 1945, Bose died in a plane crash after his overloaded Japanese plane went down, though many Indians believed that he had been killed by the British.

During the war, the British government called on Gandhi to condemn the violence that was spreading across India. He refused, saying that the violence was the outcome of Britain's severe reaction to the Quit India movement. In February 1943, Gandhi began a fast in prison as part of his peaceful protest. Hundreds of other prisoners across India emulated him. Large protests across India called for his release. The international community also joined in these calls for Gandhi's release. Influential newspapers, including the *Chicago Sun* and the *Manchester Guardian*, not only echoed these calls but also began to question the moral authority of the British Raj.

Gandhi was finally released from prison in May 1944. His health had declined sharply as a result of his fasting, and the British government was afraid of the reaction if he were to die. While a freed Gandhi was a problem, a martyred Gandhi could prompt a groundswell of outrage that might completely destabilize India.

It wasn't just Gandhi and the Congress that attracted growing support during the war. The All-India Muslim League also grew exponentially during the war years, but unlike the Congress, the League supported the British war effort. One of the most prominent leaders of the League was Muhammad Ali Jinnah, a Muslim Indian barrister. Jinnah had originally been a member of the Congress, but he resigned in the 1920s in protest at the Congress' adoption of Satyagraha. Jinnah saw this policy as leading to anarchy.

Under the leadership of Jinnah, the League increased its membership dramatically during the war years. In 1930, the League had fewer than 2,000 members across India. By 1944, it had more than one million members, including half a million in Bengal alone. Members of the League were very concerned about what an independent India might look like. In particular, they were worried that the wishes of a Muslim minority in such a nation might be ignored.

In 1940, Jinnah first propounded what became known as the Two-Nation Theory. In simple terms, this suggested that if it were to become independent, India should become two separate nations: one with a Hindu majority and the other with a Muslim majority. Jinnah and many other Muslims believed that the notion of a single, unified India was simply not viable. Jinnah told a large rally in Lahore, "Islam and Hinduism are not religions in the strict sense of the word, but are, in fact, different and distinct social orders and it is a dream that the Hindus and Muslims can ever evolve a common nationality." In contrast, Gandhi and the Congress were completely opposed to the creation of one or more states based on religion. They wanted to see a single Indian nation incorporating all three religions: Hindus, Muslims, and Sikhs.

By the time World War II finally ended in August 1945, it was becoming increasingly clear that the British Raj could not continue much longer. However, no one was entirely clear about what an India provided with self-rule might look like. Would it be a single, secular state or a number of separate states, each with a majority of a particular religion? The future was unclear and beset by some fundamental and seemingly unanswerable questions.

Chapter Ten

Independence and Partition

"Any idea of a united India could never have worked and in my judgment it would have led us to terrific disaster. Maybe that view is correct; maybe it is not; that remains to be seen."

—Muhammad Ali Jinnah

In July 1945, following the end of World War II in Europe, a general election was held in Britain. During the war, a coalition government led by Winston Churchill had led the nation. Churchill had been massively popular as a war leader, and many expected the Conservative Party he led to win the election. Instead, the people of Britain voted for change. The Labour Party, under the leadership of Clement Atlee, won a landslide victory, taking almost 50% of the popular vote as opposed to the Conservative Party's 40%. This gave the Labour Party an outright majority in

Parliament (the first time the party had achicved this) and allowed Atlee to begin to introduce a number of significant post-war reforms.

At home, these changes included important social reforms that led, amongst other things, to the creation of the National Health Service, under which, for the first time, every person in Britain could receive free health care. Atlee was also regarded as an expert on India. As early as 1934, he had advocated for giving India the same dominion status already provided to Canada. He was also aware of and sympathetic to the views of the Indian National Congress and the Muslim League.

The Labour Party election manifesto in 1945 included a commitment to "the advancement of India to responsible self-government," though it did not specifically mention independence. In this view, Atlee was completely opposed to Churchill and the Conservatives. Atlee had served as deputy prime minister under Churchill in the wartime coalition government, and the two had clashed more than once on the subject of India. Atlee's views on India were part of a larger belief in decolonization. Under the Labour government elected in 1945, Britain would begin to grant independence to areas it had formerly ruled in Africa, South East Asia, the Middle East, and China.

One of the most pressing reasons for this drive for decolonization was economic. Although it had been victorious in two world wars, Britain was left with staggering debts. After borrowing heavily during both wars, Britain had a national debt of around £21 billion in 1945. Maintaining the military and naval resources needed to protect a huge empire was simply beyond the capacity of the nation, especially as Atlee wanted to introduce costly new social reforms at home. Even before Atlee became prime minister, he had planned to offer India dominion status no later than 1948. However, he soon began to believe that full independence made more sense for both Britain and India.

The viceroy of India at the time Atlee was elected was Field Marshal Archibald Wavell. Appointed by Churchill, Wavell was opposed to independence and willfully ignorant of political developments in India. Almost as soon as he became prime minister, Atlee appointed a new and more moderate viceroy, Lord Mountbatten, and formed a cabinet mission with the prime objective of defining what form a peaceful transition to independence might take. However,

Atlee and the cabinet mission were faced with a seemingly intractable problem: Gandhi and the Congress wanted a single, unified Indian state, while Jinnah and the League wanted two separate nations based on religious majority.

In an attempt to settle this question, an election was held in India in December 1945. Rather than providing an answer, this simply confirmed existing divisions; the Indian National Congress took 59 governmental seats in the election, while the All-India Muslim League took 30. The cabinet mission suggested that India might become a single nation, but with Muslim-majority areas given some level of self-rule within this. While the Muslim League agreed to this suggestion, the Congress rejected it completely.

In response, Muslims took to the street and began to demonstrate. Some of these demonstrations became violent and led to attacks on Hindus, who, in turn, reacted with violence against Muslims. In Calcutta, over 4,000 people died during several weeks of violent confrontation, an event that became known as the Great Calcutta Killing of 1946. Fearing that the violence might spread across India and might even lead to a full-scale civil war, the Congress agreed to consider the partition of India into two separate nations, one with a Muslim majority and the other with a Hindu majority (though Gandhi himself remained opposed to this solution).

In 1947, the Partition Council was created to consider what the two nations might be. Provinces that were predominantly Hindu and Sikh were to become the nation of India, while provinces that were mainly Muslim would become the new nation of Pakistan. Some of the larger provinces which had mixed populations, including Punjab and Bengal, were to be split between the two new countries. When this was announced, violence, particularly in Bengal and Punjab provinces, escalated. Britain did not have the military resources needed to quell this violence, and fearing civil war, Viceroy Mountbatten announced that the transfer of power had to be complete by no later than June 1947.

Finally, on August 15, 1947, two entirely new nations were created. The Dominion of Pakistan (later to become the Islamic Republic of Pakistan) had Muhammad Ali Jinnah as its governor-general. The Dominion of India (later the Republic of India) had Jawaharlal Nehru as the prime minister. This day formally marked the end of the British Raj but not the end of violence and anarchy in the two countries.

In many areas, people were largely unaffected by the transition. However, in border areas between Muslim and Hindu territories, refugees began to stream in both directions. Up to twenty million people were forced to relocate in what has been described as the greatest refugee crisis of the twentieth century. Violence erupted on a scale never seen before. No one is certain how many people died between 1947 and 1949, but estimates suggest around one million. Recent investigations using census data suggest that anything up to three million people went "missing" from the Punjab alone in this period.

Appalled by this violence, Mahatma Gandhi went to the city of New Delhi in early 1948 in an effort to restore calm. At around five pm on January 30, Gandhi was about to lead a multi-faith prayer meeting in the compound of a large mansion in the city, something he had done for several days. As he walked to the podium to address the crowd, a young man ran forward and shot him three times. Gandhi died within minutes. The Indian prime minister, Jawaharlal Nehru, echoed the feelings of the whole nation when he said, "The light has gone out of our lives, and there is darkness everywhere."

Gandhi's assassin was Nathuram Vinayak Godse, a Hindu Nationalist and a member of an extreme right-wing paramilitary group, the Rashtriya Swayamsevak Sangh. Godse claimed that he had killed Gandhi because he had been too willing to accommodate Muslims during the violence of 1947/1948. Godse was executed for his crime in November 1949. Neither Gandhi nor Godse lived to see the creation of the Republic of India in 1950.

Conclusion

The British Raj was seen by many British people as a benevolent administration that brought civilization and unity to the many states that populated the Indian subcontinent in 1858. In some ways, direct British rule may have been a step up from the previous government of the East India Company, but for many ordinary Indian people, the Raj brought little in the way of concrete improvement.

It should not be forgotten that the principal mission of the Raj was to provide economic and trading benefits to the British Empire, not to improve the lot of the Indian people. This is most clearly illustrated by events such as the famines that afflicted this country during the Raj. Major famines in the second part of the nineteenth century killed up to 10 million people in India. In part, these deaths were caused by a refusal on the part of the British administration to provide relief for the victims or even to slow the export of food from India to Britain.

The huge number of casualties and vast debt that Britain incurred during World War I seriously weakened the Empire. Now, Britain simply did not have the resources needed to enforce its rule on territory scattered across the globe. In India, Britain was forced to accept some measure of self-rule through the enactment of the Government of India Act in 1935. Then, by 1939, Britain was involved in another world war that left it even weaker. This, combined with the election of Clement Atlee when that war ended, meant that it was clear that the Raj must soon come to an end.

At first, many people in Britain believed that India might become a new dominion—semi-independent but still a part of the Empire. However, the Hindu/Muslim violence that followed the first attempts to define this dominion was so widespread that British troops were unable to suppress it. The unseemly haste with which Britain withdrew from India in 1947 was an indicator of just how weak the Empire had become and a factor in the tragic violence that followed. The final and sudden end of the British Raj proved just as harmful to the people of India as its long rule had been.

Though the violence and refugee crisis had subsided by 1950, the Republic of India was beset by problems in its early years, including widespread poverty, overpopulation, and continuing independence movements in some provinces and former princely states. While some of these issues still remain, progress has been made, and today, India is the most populous democracy in the world and the world's sixth-largest economy.

For its part, Pakistan became an independent republic in 1956, but it has endured a troubled history. Attempts to create democracy in this country proved difficult, with a series of military leaders taking power up to 1970, when the first democratic elections were held. However, the army refused to hand over power, leading to a civil war where Bengali Mukti Bahini forces in eastern Pakistan began an insurgency. As a result, this region became the independent nation of Bangladesh in 1971. Relations between Pakistan and India meanwhile continued to be difficult and erupted into full-scale war on three occasions—in 1965, 1971, and 1999. It is only relatively recently that Pakistan has successfully tackled widespread poverty and begun to build a stable economy.

The end of the British Raj was directly responsible for the creation of the Republic of India and the Islamic Republic of Pakistan and indirectly for the creation of Bangladesh. These nations have experienced difficulty and many challenges, but at least since 1947, they have had the right to determine their own futures.

Bibliography

Gilmour, D. (2018). *The British in India: A Social History of the Raj*.

Hibbert, C. (1980). *Great Mutiny: India 1857*.

James, L. (2000). *Raj: The Making and Unmaking of British India*.

Tharoor, S. (2016). *An Era of Darkness: The British Empire in India*.

Printed in Great Britain
by Amazon